Puppet Shows
Made Easy!

By Nancy Renfro

Photographs by Nancy Scanlan
Illustrations by Ellen Scott Turner and Nancy Renfro

Nancy Renfro Studios
Austin, Texas

To Irma, Ruth and Martin
Puppet partners three, who
visited the make-believe of
the theater with me

Other Books published by Nancy Renfro Studios
Puppetry In Education Series

PUPPET CORNER IN EVERY LIBRARY

PUPPETRY AND THE ART OF STORY CREATION

PUPPETRY AND CREATIVE DRAMATICS IN STORYTELLING

PUPPETRY AND EARLY CHILDHOOD EDUCATION

MAKE AMAZING PUPPETS (Learning Works)

POCKETFUL OF PUPPETS (Series)

(Can be obtained from address below)

Write for free catalogue

ISBN 0-931044-13-8

Published in the United States of America by
Nancy Renfro Studios 1117 W. 9th Street, Austin Texas 78703

**Cover and inside photographs by Nancy Scanlan
In collaboration with Listening Library**

A Special Thanks!

• Tim Ditlow and the Listening Library for expressing enthusiasm for this book and making available a filmstrip of the same title that brings the ideas fully to life (see back inside cover).

• Nancy Scanlan, superb photographer, for taking the many photographs throughout.

• Forest Miner, staff member of Listening Library, for her supervision and artistic direction in coordinating the photographs.

• Celeste Cromack for serving as editor and general consultant.

• Debbie Sullivan who created many of the puppets and sets shown.

• Ellen Scott Turner for her adept illustrations.

• Nicole Cody and Mark Osborne, our child models, who share the limelight with the puppets.

TABLE OF CONTENTS

A puppet takes that brief visit into the make-believe of the theater
Plastic Bottle Magician

Introduction

This book is about creating a Wonderful World of Puppets. Puppets have magical powers. They can come alive, appear and disappear, talk, weep, laugh and dance. And a puppet can do these things better than people. It can jump higher, talk faster, weep sadder tears. It exaggerates everything and its moods change with the sky—it can be mean and villainous one moment, funny and warm the next.

A puppet can be a joyful creation in itself, or it can take that brief visit into the make-believe of the theater, combining the magic of a voice, a gesture, a sound and a tale to be told. It is here where strange, mysterious and marvelous things happen.

The ideas in this book will carry you into the realm of puppet theater and help make putting on puppet shows easier for you. With your "magic power" called *imagination,* you will find original ways to express yourself through puppets in shows that are truly your own creation, and build an entertaining repertoire of plays to captivate an audience, large or small.

Remember, the best way to put on a show is to do it—**fearlessly!** Each successive show will become easier, better coordinated and more exciting.

On With the Show!

The puppeteer is a conjurer with many tricks up the sleeve, and like a magician, is clever at creating illusions. It is these illusions that make putting on puppet shows so much fun. However, to use these techniques expertly you must begin with the Three Golden Rules—naturally!

THE THREE GOLDEN RULES

Golden Rule #1 — Think Short. It is far better to achieve a good ten to fifteen minute play than a mediocre longer one. In the beginning and until you gain expertise, concentrate on creating a superior short play. Consider combining two or three short plays, skits, or songs when a longer program is required.

Golden Rule #2 — Think Simple. This goes for *everything* in the show: the characters, scenery, props, dialogue, action and the whole caboodle. Remember that producing a show should be an enjoyable experience; if the work becomes too tedious, the fun is lost. Find inventive ways to streamline scenery and props to the bare bones, cut down on long-winded dialogue and simplify the cast.

Golden Rule #3 — Think Contrast. One of the biggest secrets in putting on an exciting show is to build into it contrast. Contrast in all aspects of a show is fun to explore and is just the trick to jolt the audience's imagination.

- Put a happy-go-lucky scene next to a melancholy scene.

- Feature a tall, lanky character with a short, chubby rascal.

- Have a character with a soft, mellow voice converse with a loud, booming character.

- Follow some fast action with some slow movement.

THE SHOW'S COMPONENTS

The chapters ahead will discuss the steps you will need to take to produce a good puppet play and to become a budding puppeteer. Now that you know the Three Golden Rules of puppet theater, you are ready to forge onward and gather the basic components for your show.

cardboard tubes

Tall and Short Characters

Here is what you will need to begin.

A Story
The Script
Puppets
Scenery
Props
The Surprises (Sound and Special Effects)
A Stage
An Audience
Imagination! (last but not least!)

Planning the Work Schedule

Plan a work schedule that will give you time to complete all of the show's components properly. A well planned schedule will help guarantee that your troupe is ready to shine in the spotlight on opening night. Short cuts and hints on simplifying construction of various items are given thorughout this book. Most important, do not spend so much time on creating the puppets and scenery that there is little time left over for developing the script and rehearsing. These elements are far more important to making a show a hit than gorgeous puppets and sets. Divide the work schedule into three parts and allow equal time to work on each segment:

1) Developing the story and script
2) Creating the set and puppets
3) Rehearsing the show

If you already know which characters are needed for the show, you may decide to create the puppets before actually writing the script, instead of after. As explained later in this chapter, the puppets are great aids in helping to actually write and visualize the script. However, if you prefer, the script can be written first and the puppets constructed after the characters are established.

Comical mushroom singing to Little Red Riding Hood
(Plastic butter dish and plastic bottle Action Style Puppet)

12

A Story

Finding a good story is the cornerstone to a successful puppet show. No matter how much effort and talent is available, it is difficult to stage a satisfactory puppet show with poor story material. In choosing a story for a show, be sure to choose one that *you* are enthusiastic about and will enjoy performing. It should revolve around characters or a theme that interests you wholeheartedly. There are several types of stories you may wish to explore.

READY-MADE STORIES

A search through bookstores or library shelves will uncover an endless selection of ready-made stories with a variety of themes. Many novice puppeteers like to begin with a fairy tale or other familiar story. "Hansel and Gretel," "Three Billy Goats Gruff" and "Little Red Riding Hood" are a few popular examples. Or, of course, you may choose a favorite modern story, one that features a monster, holiday, or other exciting theme.

FRACTURED FAIRY TALES

Fractured fairy tales are also fun to try. This is when you take a familiar tale and change it around to suit your whim. A character may speak in current slang, perhaps a twist of plot occurs, or some new cast members are added. Some offbeat ideas are suggested to get you rolling.

• *"Cinderella" could take place in an underwater setting with a sea life cast: Cinderella, played by an angel fish, the stepmother by an octopus and the stepsisters by two nagging swordfish. The story line could be modified to include sea adventures.*

• *In "Little Red Riding Hood," Little Red could meet up with some unusual characters in the forest on the way to Granny's house such as a weird monster or comical singing mushroom.*

• *Another animal could be substituted for the frog character in "The Frog Prince," such as a tarantula or mouse. Of course, retitle the story to match: "The Tarantula Prince" or "The Mouse Princess."*

Tarantula Prince

Bionic Dog

AN ORIGINAL STORY

Some of the best stories for puppet shows are those that we make up ourselves. Look around you. Listen! Let your imagination have full rein. Ideas are found in many places.

A Title (you made up)

"The Invisible _____."
"How the Giraffe Got Its Long Neck"
"The Mysterious Egg"

Sample Story Idea
"The Invisible Cat"
An invisible cat has met another invisible cat in the city. They have many, many invisible kittens. The loud, unexplained meows all over the city drive folks mad. Nobody knows how to catch the cats. A Bionic Dog is brought in and cleverly outwits the cats. (How does it catch the cats?)

A Journey (real or imaginary)

A Visit To Outer Space
An Underwater Voyage
A Visit to a Big City

Sample Story Idea
"A Visit to Outer Space"
The crew of a star ship has been asked to bring back to earth one creature from three different planets. The crew runs into difficulties on each of the planets but the creatures finally are captured, brought back to earth and featured on the TV show "That's Incredible!" (What did the creatures look like? What difficulties did the crew run into when capturing them?)

14

Creatures and Planets

Goofy Giant

A Pet Peeve

Noisy Eaters
Cutting in Line
Litterbugs

Sample Story Idea
"Noisy Eaters"
A goofy giant is taught how to eat soup properly by three different animals—a mouse, an octopus and an elephant. Each animal shows its own special technique for eating soup. The giant has to decide which is the best method for him. (What does each animal suggest?)

The Future

A Unique Animal of the Future
Discovery of a New Kind of Food
A Neat Video Game

Sample Story Idea
"Double Trouble Sonic Sodas"
A new kind of food is introduced to earth. The Master Chef Zaps is featured on television to show everyone how to make Static Sonic Sodas. It is an amazing recipe calling for some most amazing ingredients. Everyone wants to try this fantastic soda but weird results occur after drinking it, causing a great deal of trouble on Earth! (What kind of trouble does the soda cause?)

Sonic Soda

15

A vet performs emergency surgery
(puppets made from boxes)

An Object (real or imaginary)

Dog Collar
Balloon
Walking Chair

Walking Chair

Sample Story Idea

"The Walking Chair"

A dicontented chair decides to venture off to see the world. While walking down the road it grants its walking powers to other things that suddenly come to life, forming a strange and troublesome parade. (What things follow the chair?) (What trouble occurs?)

A Newspaper Clipping

An Animal Feature Story
A Sports Competition
A Rock Star's Blunder

Sample Story Idea

"The Case of the Twelve Locks"

A dog who works as a robber's assistant has a habit of swallowing locks after each robbery. He gets a severe tummy ache and is brought to the vet for emergency surgery. The vet counts twelve locks in all and becomes suspicious of its owner, the robber. (What happens to the dog?! What happens to the robber?)

These story ideas are intended to start you on the road to developing your own original puppet show. Now it's time to convert ideas into action. *Let's write a script!*

"Hansel and Gretel" opening scene—Paper Bag Action Style Puppets

★★★★★★★★★★★★★★★★★★★★★★★★★★★★★★★★★★★★

From Story to Script

With story in mind, either an existing one or one you have made up, you are ready to write the script for your puppet show. A good beginning step is to make a *Script Outline* which describes your scenes and characters.

To make it easier for you to learn how to write a script, many of the examples in this chapter are based on a familiar story, "Hansel and Gretel" to serve as a basic outline. You can use the same guidelines in this script for creating your own script outline, whether working with a fairy tale or an original story. Later the outline will be useful as a guide for designing the set and puppets as well as action.

SCRIPT OUTLINE FOR "HANSEL AND GRETEL"

A. List and describe the characters.

Woodcutter — *Sweet and humble*
Stepmother — *Nagging and coarse*
Hansel — *Meek and helpful*
Gretel — *Sassy, but easily frightened*
Witch — *Deceitful and cruel*
Jojo Bird (an additional character) — *Teasing and clownish*

B. List and describe the major scenes.

Scene #1 — The Woodcutter's House

Setting — *Late afternoon in the countryside*
Scenery — *A humble peasant cottage with adjoining vegetable garden*
Mood — *Melancholy and sad*

Scene #2 — The Forest

Setting — *The next morning at the edge of the forest*
Scenery — *Spooky trees, undergrowth and lurking eyes*
Mood — *Tense and frightening*

Scene #3 — Interior of the Witch's Candy House

Setting — *The next morning at the other end of the forest*
Scenery — *House filled with colorful, and tempting pastry and candy creations*
Mood — *Suspicious and cautious*

C. List key props.

Garden rake
Bread crumbs
Firewood and fake fire
Pastry and candy creations
Chicken bone
Cooking pot
Oven
Treasure chest of jewels

A Successful Script

Having created a Script Outline for the puppet play, you are ready to put the elements into actual script form. As a scriptwriter, strive for a happy balance between *action* and *dialogue* which will give the puppeteers a chance to show off their talents, keep the audience wide-eyed and allow the puppets to be stars.

The Action—A good puppet play should include plenty of action. A rule of thumb is *never have a puppet say something which can be easily shown (or acted out) by the puppet.* For example:

At night, a frightened Hansel suspects something is lurking in the woods behind a tree. Instead of Hansel saying, "I think I will go over and take a look behind that tree and see what is there," he could build suspense through his actions. It is much more exciting to have Hansel quietly tiptoe over to the tree, peeking back over his shoulder from time to time while nervously and cautiously looking behind the tree. How surprised your audience will be when suddenly a forest creature pops out!

The secret learned here is that you have not used dialogue to spell out exactly what was going to happen. Instead the audience followed the puppet's actions and used their imaginations to guess what was about to happen. *Anticipation* then is one of the puppeteer's best assets in building a captivating show. Learn how to use it cleverly.

The Dialogue—Another secret to good script writing is to create interesting dialogue. *Concentrate on using a variety of sentences and vary the length of speeches.* Punctuation can be fun when used with imagination to add special emphasis or indicate timing. Always keep the action in mind as you write the dialogue so that conversation will be lively. Don't bore the audience with aimless talk.

Here is a part of a successful script for "Hansel and Gretel." Note the format which helps to coordinate action and dialogue.

Hansel and Tree

Nibble, Nibble, little mouse. Who is nibbling at my house?
(Candy House with bag and box head Action Style Puppets)

Hansel and Gretel
A Partial Script

Dialogue		**Actions**
Witch:	Nibble, nibble, little mouse. Who is nibbling at my house?	*Peeks from behind the house, then suddenly pops out.*
Hansel & Gretel:	Oh... who are you?	*They jump back in surprise*
Witch:	I'm the cook. Tee, hee, hee. Er, that is I *love* to cook. Cookies cakes and candy goodies are all my specialities. Tee, hee, hee. You seem to be enjoying my cooking, dearies. Do you like it?	*Rubs hands and walks up to children while patting them on head. Turns head from side to side looking suspiciously all around.*
Gretel:	Er .. why yes, ma'am. Very good, indeed. And the windows are simply delicious.	*Nervously jumps back further. Begins to shake.*
Hansel:	Er .. yes and I especially like the roof best of all. Chocolate, isn't it? Yum, yum. Er, or is it caramel? Er .. we better go home now.	

Hansel & Gretel:		**They both turn and start to** *run.*
Witch:	Oh, no! Nonsense, my dearies. Don't go away. *Do* come in and let me show you my wonderful, *wonderful* kitchen where I make all kinds of superb and most delectable goodies—Apple Pancakes, and Cherry Tarts, Chocolate Yums Yums and Sugar Dandies. Oh, my, I am such a *superb* baker. Don't you think?	*She tugs at Hansel and Gretel to come into house.* *She shows them the kitchen*
Hansel & Gretel:	Ohhh… aren't they beautiful!	*They look over the kitchen and admire the goodies.*
Gretel:	Aren't they yummy looking?	
Hansel:	Wow — Super!	
Witch:	And my masterpiece. Oh, let me show you lucky children my pride and joy. It's what I call my grand special —the Yicky, Icky, Vanilla Vulture Creation. It has the most scrumptuous icing in the whole world.	*Brings out her Vulture Creation.*
Hansel & Gretel:	Ugh!	*Make a terrible face as they pretend to admire it.*

Vulture cake
(Paper and cardboard construction)

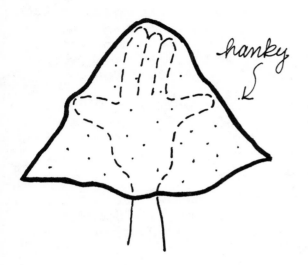

Stand-In Hanky Puppet

Most important did you notice in the script the use of long and short paragraphs? Also, there is a great variety in the punctuation. Note also that a lot of action, however subtle, occurs throughout the entire script. There will be times, of course, when the actions will be more dramatic when the story reaches its exciting moments. If you feel stumped or the ideas are not coming easily in writing the script, there are some tips which can help you:

• *Let the puppets help you.* If the puppets are not yet constructed, then use stand-in characters made from a hanky draped over your hand and secured with rubber bands as shown. You will be surprised to discover how much easier it is to think with puppets on hand, for sometimes the characters can suggest ideas. For example, put a contrasting character on each of your hands, say the Witch and Gretel. Then "think" a mean, deceiving Witch on one hand and a sweet, little girl on the other. What happens to the dialogue and actions of both characters in a situation? In surveying some pastries in the Witch's kitchen the Witch might brag, "Humph, aren't those the most delectable goodies? Hee, hee," as opposed to Gretel's comments, "Oh, my! Look at those bea-uuu-tiful pastries!" Actually seeing the puppets express these ideas makes them easier to transfer to paper.

• *Consider how many puppeteers will be performing.* This will determine how many characters and props can be onstage at one time. If there is one puppeteer, then naturally only two characters or props (two hands) can actually be operating at one time. With more puppeteers, a larger cast can be included.

• *Don't forget your sense of humor.* Even a play with a serious theme should include some humor in the plot. An audience loves to laugh and a story that makes them both laugh and cry is a memorable one!

THE OPENING

The first few minutes of any puppet show are the most critical, for they set the tone of the story as well as snare the audience. Be clever and put special pizazz into this initial aspect of the show. With a good beginning, the rest of the show is more apt to fall smoothly into place.

There are many ways a puppet show can begin, just as there are many ways to begin a storybook. You might want to study various storybooks for opening techniques. Here are some clever beginnings for "Hansel and Gretel."

• *A Narration.* "Once upon a time . . ." is an age old beginning that never fails and the audience rarely tires of hearing. It can officially mark the beginning of any show. For variety, you may wish to invent your own opening line with the dramatic flare of a news flash.

"Ladies and gentlemen. We interrupt this program to bring you a special news bulletin. There are no more trees left in any of the forests. All woodcutters are now unemployed! Please stay tuned for further developments of this terrible, terrible disaster." (A narrator can speak frontstage in full view or hidden backstage.)

• *A song.* This is a simple but sure-fire way to open up a show because everyone loves a song. Choose one to help set the appropriate mood for the show's opening. For example, Hansel and Gretel could sing, "Here We Go 'Round the Mulberry Bush" while dancing around a bush.

• *An Activity.* A show can be launched by a single activity which gradually builds up to a complete idea or *episode.* This type of activity building is one of the puppeteer's most important secrets for creating successful shows and the procedure, once learned, can be a formula for developing other activities and episodes in the story. In "Hansel and Gretel," the show could open on an activity such as the one that follows.

> *The Woodcutter begins by cultivating his garden. Then he plants a seed. After watering and tending it for a while, the seed can actually grow before the audience's eyes, making a little "pop" sound as it first appears above the ground before growing into a giant plant. Perhaps the giant plant becomes an additional character and gives corny advice to the woodcutter.*

Whichever opening you choose, it should be short and help lead into the rest of the plot. Once you have the audience's attention, you will need to introduce the conflict.

THE CONFLICT

Every good play has a conflict, or some trouble that occurs in the story. Solving the conflict adds excitement and drama to the show and involves the entire audience in the action. In "Hansel and Gretel," the conflict arises because a very poor Woodcutter who cannot afford to keep his children, foolishly submits to his nagging wife's suggestions to get rid of them. This conflict might be introduced in one of the following ways.

• *After the narrative news flash style opening previously described, the curtain could open on the Woodcutter and Stepmother discussing other job possibilities for the Woodcutter. During the discussion, he decides to test some of his skills. First as a rug beater, he discovers he is allergic to dust; then as an ice cream maker finds out he is addicted to ice cream, (of course, eating up everything he makes!) and finally, as a candlestick maker, all his candles turn out*

Woodcutter and giant plant
(Box Action Style Puppet)

crooked. At last he admits failure and allows his wife to nag him into getting rid of Hansel and Gretel.

• *Or, following the suggestion previously mentioned for opening the show with "Here We Go 'Round the Mulberry Bush," the nagging Stepmother could scold the children for idling away time and set them to work doing chores around the house. When asked to paint a fence, Hansel and Gretel make a complete mess by painting everything in sight—house, flowers, pets, etc. The impatient Stepmother flips her lid and decides then and there that the children must go!*

It is important in designing any opening scene as well as other episodes throughout the show, to search for new and offbeat ideas. Stories such as "Hansel and Gretel" are not written with a puppet show in mind. So to make it workable, don't be afraid to "stretch a tale" a bit to keep the show entertaining.

THE MIDDLE

Once the story is introduced and the conflict is presented, it is time to invent a rousing middle to unravel the plot. It is here that the conflict reaches its peak and all of the problems the characters bravely (or not too bravely) faced in the story are gradually solved. The middle will also determine how long or short your play is. Using what you have already learned in designing the show's opening episode, think of a series of similar short episodes that involve the characters and can be combined to make one longer middle. "Hansel and Gretel" might include the following middle episodes.

• *Hansel overhears the Stepmother's sneaky plans to take Hansel and Gretel into the woods and get rid of them.*

• *He secretly shows his collection of colorful pebbles to use as trail markers to Gretel so they will be able to find their way safely back home again.*

• *All three are off to the woods! The Stepmother pretends that they are to search for some mushrooms for supper. Craftily, she leaves the children behind where they spend a frightening night in the creepy woods.*

• *The next morning Hansel and Gretel happily follow the pebbles back home!*

• *The Stepmother takes them out once again, but this time Hansel cannot collect any pebbles. Hansel and Gretel spend another spooky night in the woods.*

• *Then smart thinking Hansel, tries to follow the bread crumb markers he substituted for the pebbles. Oops! Their pet Jojo Bird, uninvited, ate them all. Now they are in real trouble!*

• *Hansel and Gretel hopelessly try to find their way home and come across a most delicious candy cottage where lives a master chef, a sweet but deceitful old lady who loves to bake candies and pastries for children. They admire and taste all her wonderful goodies.*

• *Deceitful, yes! That sweet old lady is actually a Witch and quickly captures Hansel and prepares to bake him into one of her marvelous creations. She sets Gretel to work as kitchen maid.*

Now that you have jotted down all your middle episodes and adventures in sequence, concentrate on developing only one episode at a time, just as the opening episode example of the seed planting idea, planning and building upon the action and dialogue. If you concentrate hard you might find that you can actually stretch out what appears to be a short, dull episode into a much longer and more exciting one. Not all of the episodes need to be spellbinders, but a few should be and this may require extra focus and work on your part. For example, if Hansel and Gretel are spending a spooky night in the forest what are all of the things you can possibly think of that could happen to them to make this a more exciting scene?

• *The trees could begin to come alive in twisting their grotesque branches. Perhaps one could even punch the sleeping Hansel!*

• *Mysterious eyes could glow in the dark, eventually emerging as frightening beasts.*

• *A spooky moon could chant a spooky rhyme.*

• *The earth could begin to rumble and grumble, ejecting up mists of fog (baby powder) and steam (air scent atomizer) here and there.*

Once each episode is complete, link them together. Presto! The middle of the story will be written. Now you are ready to take on an ending.

THE GRAND FINALE

Do not disappoint your audience for they will want a noteworthy ending as a final memory of the show and a good time. Think of several different solutions for ending the show and, of course, solving the conflict, before settling on one.

What are the possible endings for "Hansel and Gretel?"

• *When asked to light the oven, Gretel pretends she does not know how. The Witch demonstrates how to light the oven step-by-step and is unexpectedly shoved into the oven by Gretel. Gretel releases the captive Hansel and together they find wonderful hidden treasures in the house. Happily, they return to the father and learn the Stepmother has left home. The three live in riches and vow they will never part again. (This is the traditional version ending.)*

• *Gretel is asked by the Witch to bake bread. As Gretel mixes up a huge bowl of batter, she pushes the Witch into the batter and bakes her in the oven. The bread comes out in the form of a Witch. After releasing Hansel, they enter their fantastic Witch bread creation at the State Fair and win a big money prize which they give to their father when they return home. (This is a made-up version.)*

After you are "pleased as punch" with the script, let different members of the group read the parts out loud. Ask for any suggestions to improve it, always feeling free to make changes towards refining the script, *anytime,* even up to the final performance!

Now you are ready to build the show.

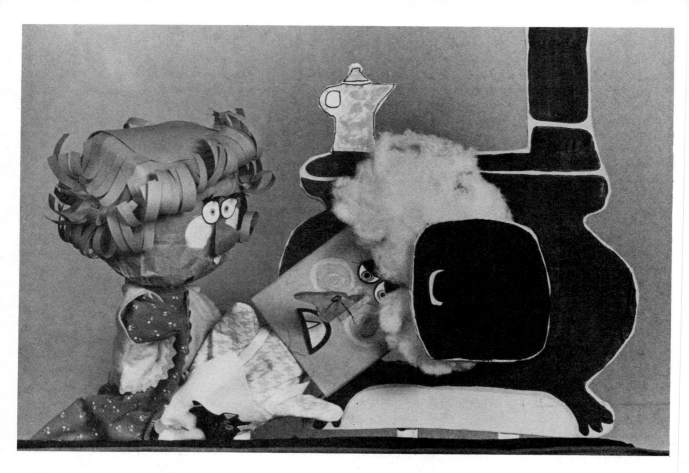

Gretel pushes witch into oven
(traditional ending)

Gretel receives award for prize witch bread
(untraditional ending)

Plastic odds and ends Robot wth toy Rocketship

Building the Show

You can put as much or as little work into building the puppets, scenery, props and sound track as you wish. Even the simplest puppet and a few ready-made props (with the aid of that light bulb flashing over your head), can be the components for a smashing show hit. The amount of time invested in the actual assembling of the show is purely a personal choice.

MATERIALS AND TOOLS

It will be helpful to round up some basic materials and tools for general construction in making sets and puppets.

Basic Materials and Tools

- *Scissors*
- *White liquid glue, paste or other glue*
- *Colored construction paper*
- *Stapler and staples*
- *Scotch tape and masking tape*
- *Crayons, felt-tip marker pens, and tempera, flat latex wall or acrylic tube paint*
- *Paintbrush*

Of special interest to the blossoming puppet maker and set builder is the value of stocking up on some basic colors in flat latex wall paint. This wonderful paint, obtained at the paint store has superb coating powers and durability. It is also cheaper than tempera paint and because of its thickness, goes further. Consider obtaining a quart each of the primary colors (red, blue and yellow) black, white and a basic flesh one. Other colors can be easily mixed from this basic stock.

Bonus Items

In addition to these basic items, there are several tools and materials which are worth the investment and are a bonus to the puppet maker. Most of these items can be obtained at a hardware store.

• *A sturdy hand-grip type stapler,* similar to those used in check-out counters at stores is recommended. An excellent model is the "Arrow" brand #P-22 found in most hardware stores. This stapler manages hard to reach areas and has extra long staples for superior stapling of heavyweight papers and cardboards.

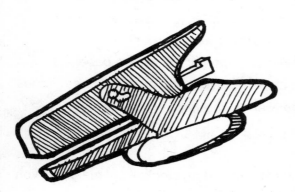

Hand Grip Stapler

33

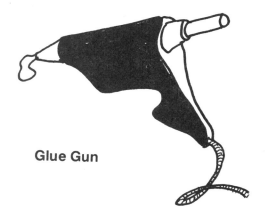

Glue Gun

• *An electric glue gun,* available at most hardware stores, is a must for any adult who works regularly in crafts. When plugged in, the glue gun melts a small nylon pellet which is then applied to the surfaces to be glued, forming a high strength joint. It is invaluable as a substitute for sewing chores as well as general gluing. This tool requires handling with extreme care to avoid contact of the hot material on the fingers. **This tool should be used only by adults.**

• *A tube of double barrel epoxy or other strong glue* is another useful material to have on hand for gluing difficult items such as metal or plastic.

• *Wide silver duct tape* is an extra strong tape that will be indispensible to the puppeteer who will find 1001 uses for holding together props, puppetry, scenery, etc.

Treasure Bin

Another asset for the puppeteer is to collect a treasure bin of odds and ends found around the house. This will spark imagination in designing the sets and puppets and could include items such as those listed below.

—*Boxes of various sizes: spaghetti, oatmeal, pudding, cake mix, and detergent*

—*Egg cartons*

—*Old sheets*

—*Paper towel, bathroom tissue or other cardboard tubes*

—*Plastic "bubbles" and styrofoam packing shapes, shipping boxes*

—*Aluminum foil and plastic food wrap*

—*Tissue paper, fancy holiday wrapping paper and ribbons*

—*L'eggs® hosiery containers*

—*Paper plates, cups, drinking straws and ice cream or Popsicle® sticks*

—*Sequins, beads and old jewelry*

—*Scrap fabric, yarns, buttons and trims*

—*Wallpaper and rug samples (available at stores)*

—*Foam rubber (available at upholstery shops)*

—*Gummed reinforcements for looseleafe paper*

—*Gummed or self-adhesive stars, dots, or other shapes*

—*String, rubber bands and paper fastener brads*

—*Dowels or sticks*

Now that you have an interesting stockpile of materials you can begin building your show.

Fabric

Yarn

Egg Carton

Drinking Straws

Cardboard Tube

SUPER CEREAL

SPAGETTI

Gum Reinforcers and Stars

SOAP

Food Boxes

Plastic Bottles

THE PUPPETS

The most popular puppets used for shows are hand puppets. They are easy to manipulate and are great hams when it comes to expressing actions, gestures and dialogue.

Investigate the two types of hand puppets, the Talking *Mouth* and *Action Style puppets,* described below to determine which is most suitable for your production. You might like to have some characters from each style. The Talking Mouth Puppet with its flexible mouth would certainly be fitting for a nagging Stepmother or singing pizza; while the Action Style Puppet is more suitable for Hansel or Gretel or a busy chef who perform many actions. Whatever puppet types you settle on, check the finished puppet for comfort and fit. If the puppet's head is too heavy, too loose, or too tight over the hand, the puppeteer will not be able to operate it smoothly.

In creating puppets keep in mind that felt punctures easily and is not recommended to use for parts of a puppet that takes lots of wear and tear unless it is lined with another material. There are many find modern fabrics such as double-knits and polyester blends to try instead. Also try some of the super new polyester type felts such as Phel Phun and Polyfelt which are stronger than felt and washable. Make a search in the fabric shot for interesting puppet making materials.

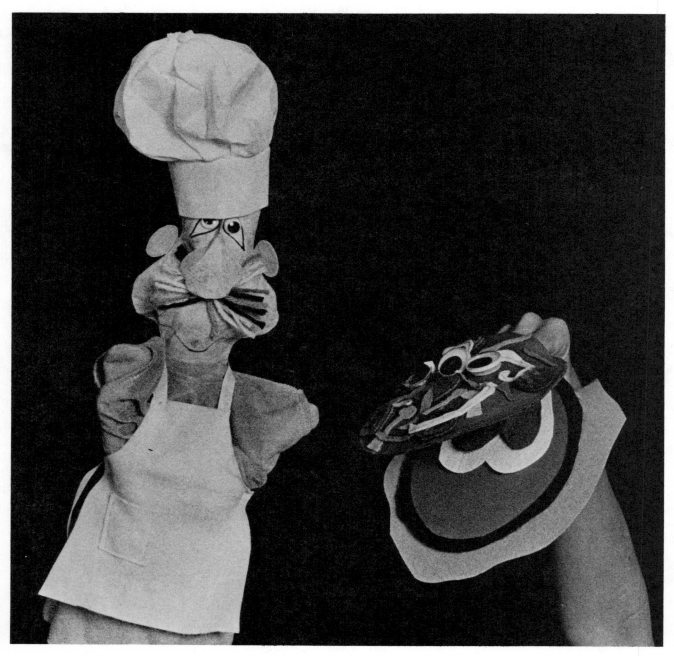

Chef Pellon Action Style and Pizza Talking Mouth Puppet

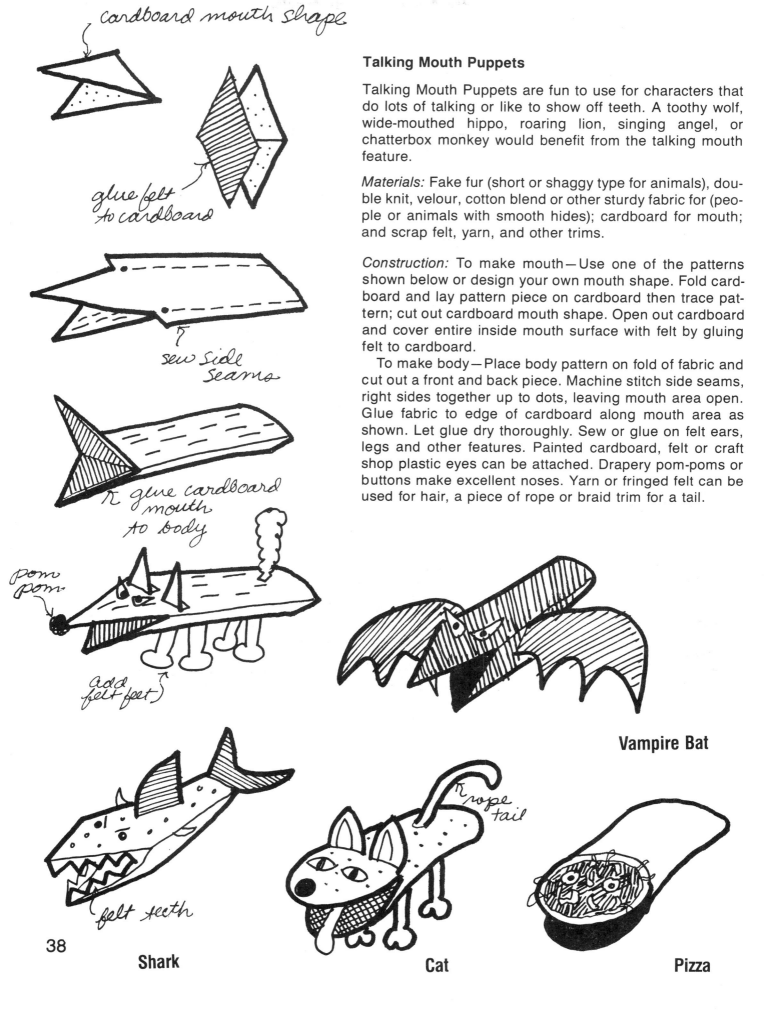

cardboard mouth shape

glue felt to cardboard

sew side seams

glue cardboard mouth to body

pom pom

add felt feet

Talking Mouth Puppets

Talking Mouth Puppets are fun to use for characters that do lots of talking or like to show off teeth. A toothy wolf, wide-mouthed hippo, roaring lion, singing angel, or chatterbox monkey would benefit from the talking mouth feature.

Materials: Fake fur (short or shaggy type for animals), double knit, velour, cotton blend or other sturdy fabric for (people or animals with smooth hides); cardboard for mouth; and scrap felt, yarn, and other trims.

Construction: To make mouth—Use one of the patterns shown below or design your own mouth shape. Fold cardboard and lay pattern piece on cardboard then trace pattern; cut out cardboard mouth shape. Open out cardboard and cover entire inside mouth surface with felt by gluing felt to cardboard.

To make body—Place body pattern on fold of fabric and cut out a front and back piece. Machine stitch side seams, right sides together up to dots, leaving mouth area open. Glue fabric to edge of cardboard along mouth area as shown. Let glue dry thoroughly. Sew or glue on felt ears, legs and other features. Painted cardboard, felt or craft shop plastic eyes can be attached. Drapery pom-poms or buttons make excellent noses. Yarn or fringed felt can be used for hair, a piece of rope or braid trim for a tail.

Vampire Bat

felt teeth

rope tail

Shark

Cat

Pizza

38

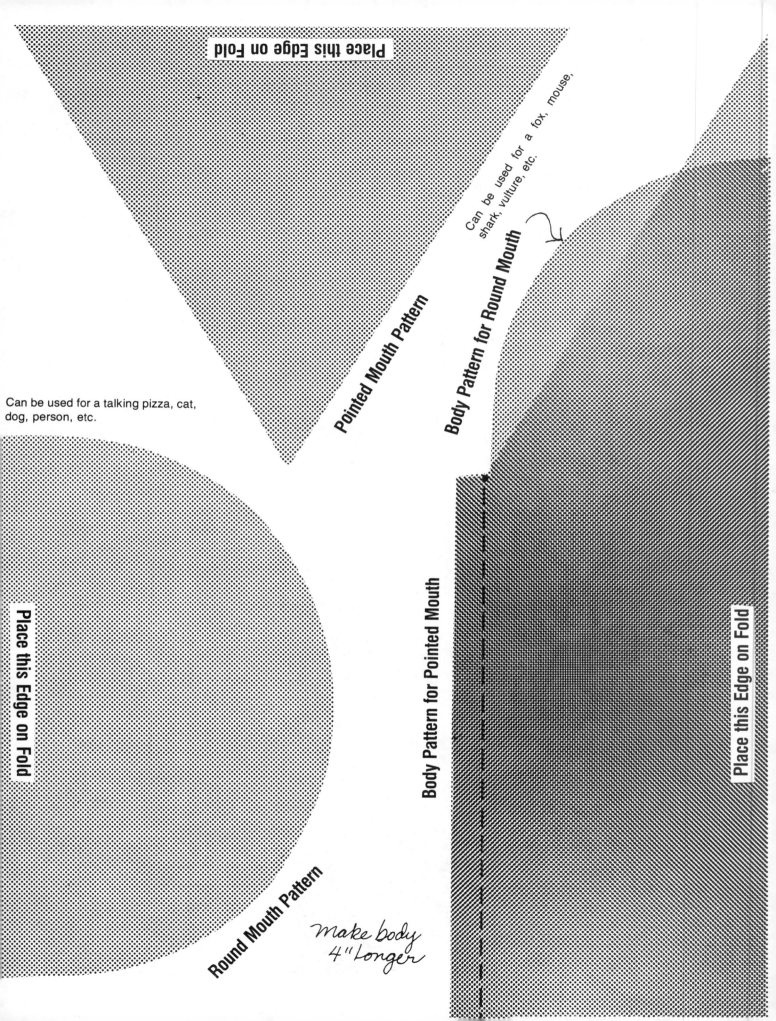

Place this Edge on Fold

Pointed Mouth Pattern

Can be used for a talking pizza, cat, dog, person, etc.

Can be used for a fox, mouse, shark, vulture, etc.

Body Pattern for Round Mouth

Body Pattern for Pointed Mouth

Place this Edge on Fold

Place this Edge on Fold

Round Mouth Pattern

Make body 4" Longer

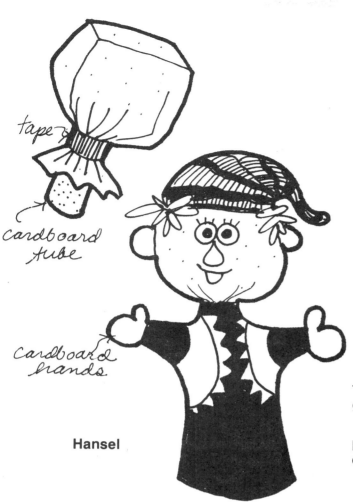

tape

cardboard
tube

cardboard
hands

Hansel

Action Style Puppets

Action Style Puppets can do amazing things. Because they have arms that are designed for movement, they have the ability to sweep a floor with a broom, pick up objects, or turn pages of a book. The Action Style Puppet is perfect to portray a chef whipping up cake batter, a baseball player at bat, a strong man lifting weights, or a ballerina twirling pirouettes.

Several types of Action Style Puppet Construction follow.

• *Basic Paper Bag Head*

Materials: Small paper bag; newspaper; short cardboard tissue tube; fabric; construction paper; and scrap felt, yarn, and other trims.

Construction: Firmly stuff paper bag 3/4 full with crumpled newspaper.

— Poke tube up inside bag. Squeeze neck of bag around tube and wrap masking tape around entire neck. A dab of glue on the tube will help hold tube in place.

— Paint head if desired or leave natural. When dry, add paper, cardboard or felt features. Yarn, cotton, or fringed construction or tissue paper or fabric make excellent hair.

— See instructions on page 43 to add body.

Strongman Paper Bag Puppet with variation on construction.

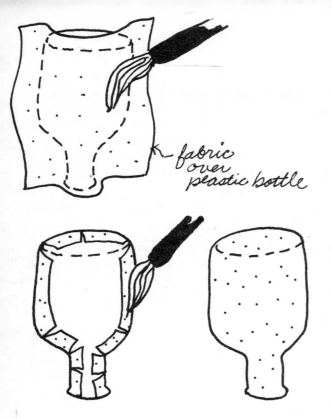

fabric over plastic bottle

Note: Latex Wall Paint will stick directly to plastic bottles without any preparation or fabric covering. Consider buying a basic flesh tone for all around use.

- *Plastic Bottle Head*

Materials: Small or medium-sized plastic bottle (detergent, shampoo, lotion); old sheet, muslin or other solid cotton fabric; and scrap felt, yarn and other trims.

Construction: Wash bottle thoroughly. Be sure neck of bottle fits comfortably over finger. (If not cut neck of bottle off to improve fit.)

— With a paint brush, coat one side of the bottle with a layer of diluted white glue (mix one part water with two parts glue).

— Lay a piece of sheeting or cotton fabric, cut slightly larger than the half bottle area, over wet glue surface as shown.

— Paint another layer of diluted glue over top of fabric until entirely soaked; smooth fabric down with brush tip.

— Trim off edge of fabric all around the bottle near the half way line, leaving a 1/2 inch margin of overhanging fabric all around. Clip fabric at corners of bottles as shown.

— With brush, dab glue on overhanging fabric edges. Smooth edges down around bottle with brush tip; let dry.

— Cover opposite side of bottle in same manner.

— When dry, paint head and add features. Felt or cardboard cutouts can be added for building up features such as ears and eyes. Plastic cosmetic bottle caps or buttons make perfect noses. Add yarn, cotton, and fringed paper or fabric for hair. Paint on a mouth, eyelashes and other details.

— See instructions on page 43 to add body.

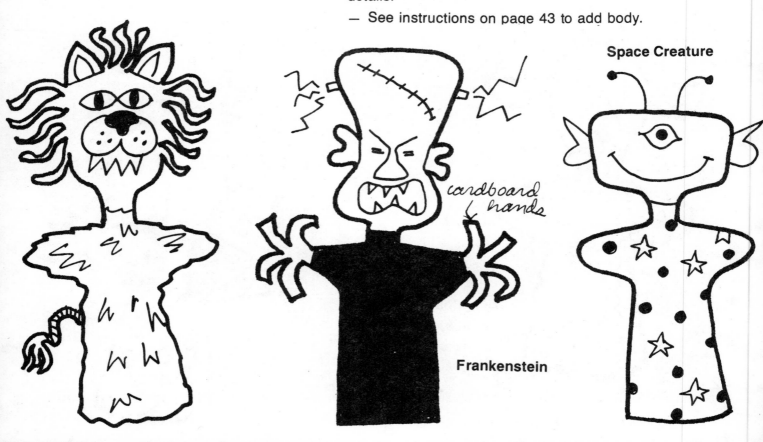

cardboard hands

Frankenstein

Space Creature

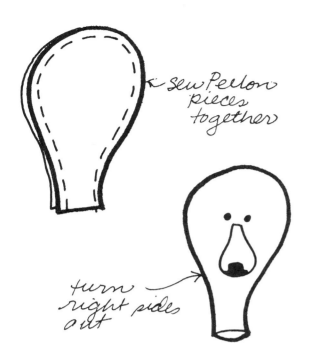

sew Pellon pieces together

turn right sides out

• *Basic Pellon Head*

Materials: Heavyweight white Pellon (interlining material obtained at fabric shop); cardboard; and scrap felt, yarn, and other trims.

Construction: Use the basic pattern below or design your own head shape. Cut out a front and back head piece.

— Line up pieces, right sides together, and sew around edges leaving neck sections open; turn right sides out. Use a pencil as an aid to poke fabric right sides out.

— Outline features such as eyes and mouth on Pellon with a dark felt-tip marker pen. Color in features and rest of face area with crayons or felt-tip marker pens.

— Complete head by sewing or gluing yarn, cotton or fringed felt hair in place.

See instructions on page 43 to add body. Matching Pellon fabric can be used for body for this puppet. Also color with crayon or felt-tip marker pens.)

felt ears

Billy Goat

felt nose

Troll

42

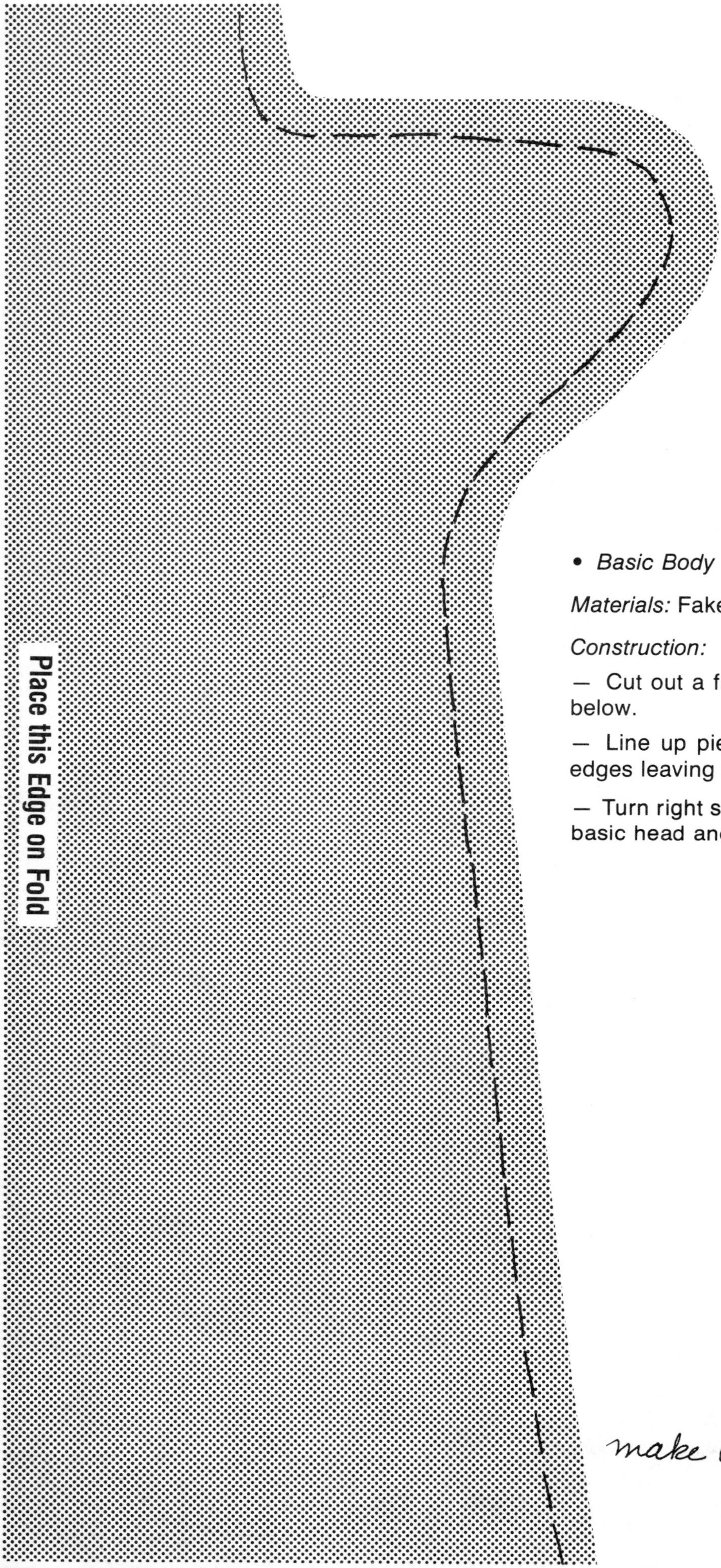

• *Basic Body*

Materials: Fake fur, double-knit, felt, cotton or other fabric.

Construction:

— Cut out a front and back body piece following pattern below.

— Line up pieces and sew right sides together, around edges leaving neck and bottom sections open.

— Turn right sides out and slip neck opening over neck of basic head and sew or glue in place. Hem bottom.

make body 2" longer

Stuffed Toy

Puppet Stand-Ins

Not all of the characters in a show need be elaborately constructed, especially the unimportant ones or those who spend only a short amount of time onstage. Here are some suggestions for making instant casts to stand in for puppets.

• *Stuffed toys* make good substitutes for puppets. Plush toy animals, novelty toys, soft sculpture dolls and other similar items can quickly be called to make stage appearances. Remove the stuffing of the toy and insert hand inside to use as a hand puppet.

• *Stick characters* can be assembled by attaching picture images or items to sticks or dowels. A drawing, magazine, greeting card or poster picture can easily be transformed into cast members. Novelty items found in toy or party shops such as a plastic skeleton, spider or astronaut can also be attached to sticks. For a large cast, try grouping characters together by drawing them on one picture and attaching to one stick control. A flock of lambs, school of fish or cheering crowd of people can be done this way.

• *Real People* also make great stand-ins for cast and can dramatize scale in an exciting way. The giant in "Jack and the Beanstalk" played by a person, the Witch in "Hansel and Gretel," or Santa Claus in a Christmas story could be fun to try.

Novelty Toy on Stick

Person with Mask

Nervous Mouse

When your acting cast is complete, you are ready to move on. It is time to bring your puppets to life!

THE PUPPET'S PERSONALITY

Making the puppet is only half the fun, creating a unique personality for the puppet is the other half. Try to develop personalities that will intrigue your audience—a stiff-jointed robot that constantly goes haywire; a dainty, squealing little mouse who scampers nervously about; and a conniving, jewel thief with a nervous tick. Once the puppet is constructed, boldly set forth to model its personality in any way you wish. Here are some ways to reveal your puppet's personality.

• *Give it a voice.* You probably have lots of voices you didn't know existed: high, low, sweet and mean, among others. Study your puppet and try to match the right voice to it. Try this simple voice exercise by reciting the following poem in a normal voice.

> *Roses are red,*
> *Violets are blue,*
> *If I were a puppet,*
> *I'd flip somersaults for you!*

Now repeat the same poem as if you were a

—*pompous king.*

—*tiny little mouse.*

—*very sleepy hippopotamus.*

—*feeble old man.*

—*cackly, wicked wtich.*

—*mechanical, jerky robot.*

Can you think of some other voices to try?

• *Discover the way your puppet moves.* A puppet's movements can make it a more interesting character. Try out postures, gestures and gaits to find the ones which reflect your puppet's personality.

—*The regal king could walk with chin in air and chest puffed out.*

—*The mouse could skitter about with short, quick runs.*

—*The old man might hobble along with small, shaky motions.*

—*The witch could dart swiftly about as if always on a broom.*

—*The robot could walk in a linear pattern with mechanical jerks.*

Feeble Old Man

• *Think up an idiosyncrasy for your puppet.* This distinguishing feature will complete the puppet's personality. The king could tug at his beard, the mouse constantly bump into things and the robot occasionally make sputtering sounds when exasperated. Or, in our sample story of "Hansel and Gretel," the Woodcutter can be absentminded or the Witch constantly smacking her lips. It is these things that will make the character more endearing to you and the audience.

Now that you have a fully rounded personality, your puppet is ready to make its grand debut.

ACTING WITH PUPPETS

Puppets are natural hams. They love to act and to be in the limelight. Like any other skill, acting with puppets takes practice. Plan to spend some time getting to know your puppet better before performing. A wall mirror is useful when practicing since it lets you see how the puppet is behaving. Good puppet actors will benefit from the following hints.

• *Holding the puppet.* If you are using an Action Style type hand puppet there are three methods of holding the puppet. Experiment with the puppet to find the best finger position for you.

Method 1   **Method 2**   **Method 3**

  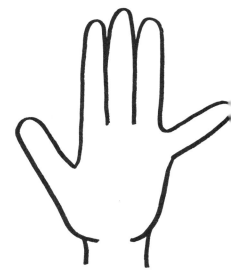

• *Think energy.* If you are tired and listless, so too, will be your puppet (and the audience will take notice). Only practice when you are feeling full of pep for the best results. Don't let the puppet rest or lean against the stage. No one can possibly feel energetic when leaning against a wall; this includes puppets!

• *Establish good posture.* A puppet should never bend over or appear "droopy" unless it is supposed to behave that way. Also, be careful that the puppet does not sink below the level of the stage. Keep the puppet straight at all times and work with the full height of its body.

Good Posture   **Poor Posture**

• *Make the puppet's movements count.* Beware of puppets suffering from "jigolitis," or unnecessary movement. Puppets that bounce around without reason, soon become boring actors. Let every action be meaningful. Plan each movement or gesture to go with a particular dialogue or idea. Observe theater and television actors to learn more about good movements and gestures. Also, learn to "freeze" your puppet; that is, make it remain perfectly still when another puppet is talking or acting. Two puppets moving at the same time onstage is confusing to the audience.

If you keep these hints in mind, you will soon be amazed to discover the many feats your puppet can do onstage. As a warm up, can your puppet do all these interesting things?

—*Wave to the audience.*

—*Clap hands.*

—*Clap hands to a rhythm.*

—*Jump up and down.*

—*Walk happily in the sunshine.*

—*Walk droopily in the rain.*

—*Jog around a track.*

—*Look for something the puppet lost.*

—*Read a book.*

—*Pick up pebbles.*

—*Dust a room with a feather duster.*

—*Mix up some cake batter.*

—*Do a circus trick.*

—*Stretch, yawn and go to bed.*

—*Bow to the audience!*

Reading a Book

A Dance

What else can your puppet do?

If you have fellow puppeteers, see what two puppets can achieve.

—*Go around the mulberry bush.*

—*Have a race.*

—*Do a dance together (rock, square, or other).*

—*Have a tug of war.*

—*One puppet can try to scare another.*

—*One puppet can cheer another puppet who is sad.*

Or try using a prop with your puppet.

—*Clean a room with a feather duster* (as if you hated housework; as if you loved housework).

—*Mix a cake with a plastic bowl and spoon.*

—*Write a letter with a pen and paper* (to someone you love; to someone you hate).

—*Have one character scrub another character's back with a scrub brush.*

—*Have a tug of war with a rope.*

—*Catch a fly with a fly swatter.*

Now have the puppets try some of these more advanced activities that express emotions.

—A puppet is very sad because she wants to see the movie *Star Trek III* but has no money. She walks very sadly across the stage. Suddenly she spies a five dollar bill on the ground, picks it up and runs happily off.

—A puppet sits down to think (taps forehead), gets a great idea (pops up in joy), runs over to another puppet and whispers the idea in secret. They both show great joy.

—A puppet is trapped in a spooky cave. He is very worried and starts to pace back and forth. He hears strange noises and trembles. Now he is terrified. Suddenly another puppet pops out and taps the first puppet who faints dead away.

A superb book and lots of ideas for learning to act with puppets is *Making Puppets Come Alive* by Larry Engles and Carol Fijan (order from Puppeteers of America Bookstore, P.O. Box 3128, Santa Ana CA 92703).

Having mastered such skills, your puppet is ready to "break a leg!" (A theatrical expression for success on the opening night performance.)

Plastic bottle head Action Style Puppet with feather duster prop.

Plastic Bottle Action Style Pig and Talking Mouth Wolf Puppet.

Painted background for a spooky Halloween set

Plastic sandwich bag ghost on a stick

Futuristic Scene

Desert Scene

DESIGNING THE SET

A scene can be as simple as a single flower or as complex as a satellite city of tomorrow. As with the puppets, the choice of how much time to spend on creating the set is a personal one. Fancy sets are fun to build but are not necessary. One or two trees can represent a forest, a barn sets the tone for a farmyard, and a few stars or planets represent the universe. The audience's imagination will easily fill in any void of scenery.

Look back at the Script Outline to recall where the action takes place. In a city, zoo, outer space or African village? Is it morning or afternoon; the past, present or future? Close your eyes and make a mental image of your set.

Use your inventiveness in choosing scenery to highlight your show; here are some ideas to try.

• *A spooky forest in "Hansel and Gretel" could use dark, purplish colors with many shiny eyes of hidden creatures amongst the trees.*

• *A futuristic set could include lots of aluminum foil, super slick skyscrapers and twinkling lights. (Why not recycle those Christmas lights!)*

• *A dream land set could have a hazy effect with pastel colored gauzy fabric stretched across the stage.*

• *An Egyptian theme could center around a pyramid and a large sun with sandy desert and yellow, hot colors.*

Search in the library for picture books to inspire you in designing the scenery. After you visualize your set, then choose the methods which will create enchanting scenery for your show.

Background scenery—Painted background scenery sets a mood that can add reality or whimsy to your show. Mural, butcher and ordinary brown wrapping paper are all perfect for background materials. Color or paint a scenic design on the paper, such as a forest, garden, ocean or galaxy of stars with paint, felt-tip marker pens, crayons, or pastels.

A permanent background scene can be created on cotton muslin, old sheets, or heavyweight Pellon® (interfacing material). All of these materials take paint, felt-tip marker pens and crayons well. Outline your design with felt-tip marker pens first, then fill in the areas with other coloring medium. Be sure to experiment on a test swatch of fabric before proceeding with entire design. Also keep all background scenery simple and uncluttered so that the puppets stand out clearly.

Hung scenery—Items can be easily suspended with strings or wires from horizontal bars above the stage to give

your set an added dimension.

• *A row of bold paper leaves in bunches will add to the dense forest foliage for "Hansel and Gretel."*

• *Birds, clouds, rain and a sun or moon are all suited for hanging scenery.*

• *Stars and planets made from cardboard and covered with aluminum foil will create an ethereal touch for an outer space theme.*

• *A cobweb made from yarn or cording, or drawn with black felt-tip marker pen on a sheet of clear acetate or plastic bag (cut apart) can be hung from random places for an eerie set.*

• *A row of silver Christmas tinsel hung across the entire width of the middle stage suggests a rainstorm.*

• *Paper snowflake cutouts will give a snowy effect for a wintery scene.*

Cloud, Sun, Rain, Bird and Parachute

Spider and Web

Ant and Mound

Movable scenery—Scenery that can be quickly taken up and down is fun to experiment with and offers great flexibility. Notice the opportunities the puppets have to interact with such scenery.

- *A tree behind which a fox hides, then peeks out menacingly.*
- *A house for a character to appear to walk inside.*
- *A mound from which an ant can pop up.*
- *A spaceship from which a space creature appears.*
- *A stairway which characters can go up and down.*
- *A slide for a little child to slide down.*
- *A swing for a monkey to play on.*
- *A pot belly stove to cook on.*
- *A fire house for a fire engine to come out of.*
- *A tunnel for a train to chug through.*
- *An ocean wave in which a fish can splash about.*

Movable scenery pieces such as a spaceship or flower can be made quickly by cutting out pictures from posters, magazines, or drawings and mounting them to stiff cardboard for reinforcement. Or, throwaway items might be used to help build a variety of sets.

- Detergent or cereal box—*house, castle or other building.*
- Egg carton—*bumpy terrain.*
- Cardboard tube—*tree trunk, tower, post or rocketship.*
- Cardboard paint bucket or large round ice cream container—*circus tent.*
- Shoe box—*bed.*
- Small food boxes—*various furniture.*

Shoe Box Bed

If you plan to use scenery over and over again, Permanent Movable Scenery can be made by covering a basic cardboard shape with fabric. The fabric provides a durable surface that takes paint very well and gives a professional touch.

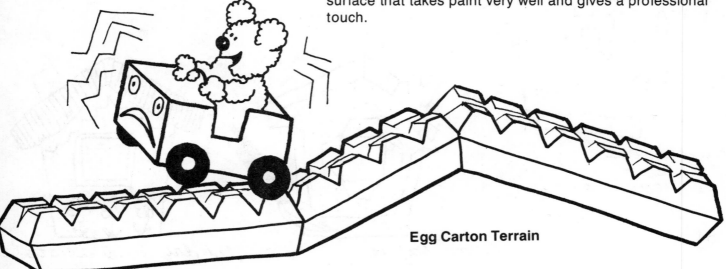

Egg Carton Terrain

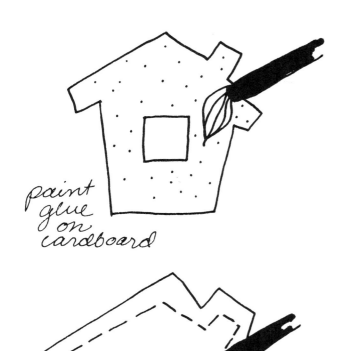

paint
glue
on
cardboard

To Make Permanent Movable Scenery

Materials: Grocery carton cardboard; diluted white glue (mix one part water with two parts white glue until it is the thickness of heavy cream); old sheet or pillow case, muslin or cotton fabric; and tempera or flat latex wall paint.

Construction:

— Draw and cut out your scenery shape from cardboard.

— With your brush, paint a layer of diluted white glue over the entire surface of the cardboard shape.

— Lay a section of fabric (larger than cardboard shape) over top of cardboard shape and wet glue.

— Paint a second layer of diluted white glue over top of fabric and smooth out fabric with tip of brush.

— Trim off the overhanging edges of the fabric on the cardboard shape, leaving a one inch wide margin all the way around; clip any corners and curves of fabric along edge as shown.

— Turn scenery shape over and paint diluted glue around edges of fabric margin. Wrap the fabric margin edges around the cardboard shape to make a smooth edge. Let dry thoroughly.

— Let completed shape dry thoroughly and paint with tempera or latex wall paint.

Scenery as previously described can be highlighted by adding three dimensional items such as colorful candy to the Witch's house in "Hansel and Gretel," a silver bell for a church or sunflower seeds to a sunflower. A neat trick to use with scenery is to Velcro® certain items to scenery such as cardboard coconuts for a monkey to pull off.

lay fabric
over cardboard

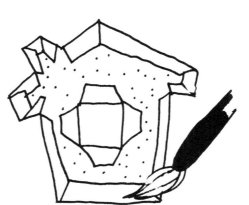

wrap fabric

let dry and decorate

trim edges
and
clip corners

Cardboard Cottage covered with fabric for permanency

Spring Clothespin Holder

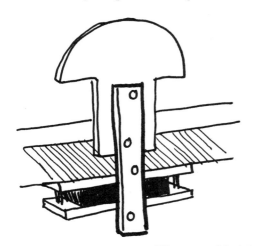

Magnet Holder

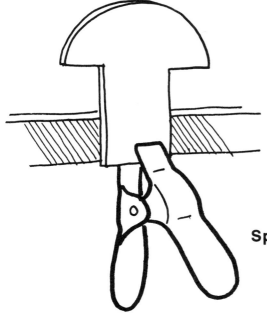

Spring Clamp Holder

Scenery Holders—There are a few clever ways Movable Scenery pieces can be attached to the stage that will be a great aid to the puppeteer in giving flexibility to the set.

• *Clothespin holder.* Glue two spring clothespins, facing upwards and approximately three inches apart, to inside edge of stage front. Bottom of scenery can be slipped into the tips of clothespins. If three dimensional scenery is used, add an extension piece of cardboard to bottom of scenery to insert in holder if necessary.

• *Magnet holder.* A series of strong magnets can be attached to front inside edge of stage with screws or epoxy. Metal plates, approximately 1¼ inches wide by 6 to 8 inches high, glued with epoxy glue or taped with silver duct tape to back of lightweight scenery pieces can be stuck to magnet with quick ease. Recommended is the D60, 528—1⅞" x ⅞"—rectangular magnet (approximately $4.00 for two magnets) purchased from Edmund Scientific Company, 101 E. Gloucester Pike, Barrington, N.J. 08007. Write for free catalog and prices from this exciting company.

• *Clamp holders.* A spring type clamp purchased at a hardware store is a firm means of holding up both light and heavy weight scenic pieces. These are suitable only if there is a framework along the front or back stage edge in which to attach the clamp.

Whatever type of scenery you are using or the method of attaching it, be sure that scenery changing is a smooth and speedy operation. Changing and arranging scenery takes practice, like any other aspect of the show, to overcome any techical problems that might arise. Take into account that you will have to transfer from one scenic set to the next and this should be done quickly or you risk losing the audience during intermission. It is far better to have a simple set that works well than a complex one that takes an octopus to manage or bogs down the production.

plastic bottle head

Rock 'n' Roller

FUN WITH PROPS

A rock and roller twangs away at a guitar, a science fiction creature blasts off in a rocket ship and a mad magician pulls out endless rabbits from a top hat. Characters using props add excitement to any show. Props have the special ability to animate and give puppets new chances for interaction. Also, they can easily be put onstage and removed at a moment's notice.

Since props are one of the puppeteer's best friends, play them to the hilt. Many episodes can be built around a key prop giving a show excitement and focus.

Props may be in proper scale with puppets or take on a humorous effect if ridiculously out of proportion. For example, the witch in "Hansel and Gretel" could mix up a cake batter with a real egg beater and bowl giving more emphasis to the props. Also, plan to use a mixture of both constructed props as well as ready-made found-object props.

Witch with egg beater prop

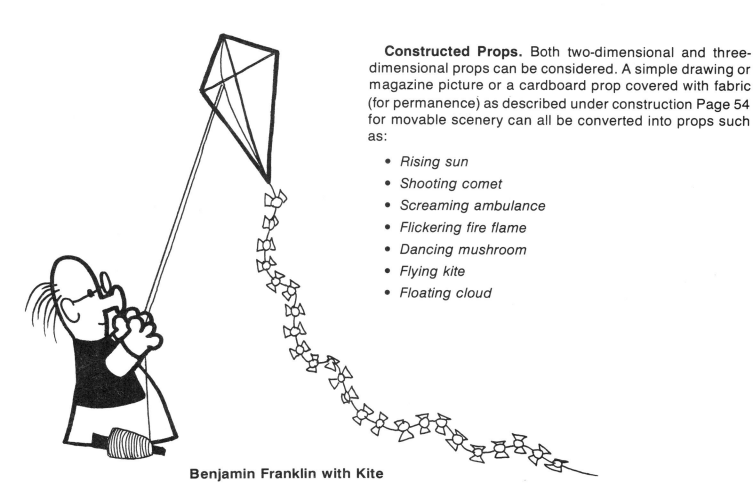

Constructed Props. Both two-dimensional and three-dimensional props can be considered. A simple drawing or magazine picture or a cardboard prop covered with fabric (for permanence) as described under construction Page 54 for movable scenery can all be converted into props such as:

- *Rising sun*
- *Shooting comet*
- *Screaming ambulance*
- *Flickering fire flame*
- *Dancing mushroom*
- *Flying kite*
- *Floating cloud*

Benjamin Franklin with Kite

58

Props made from throw away items are also intriguing, for example:

• *Car, plane, boat, spaceship, motor scooter, bicycle, wagon, fire truck, ice cream truck, circus calliope and bulldozer can be created by assembling food boxes.*

• *A video game machine with see-through control panels can be made from a large detergent or cereal box.*

• *Rake, hoe, shovel, pickax, or other tool can be made from dowels combined with cardboard shapes.*

Box Video Games

Cheese Grater Prop

Found-Object Props. A scavenger hunt around the house or garage sales will uncover some interesting ready-made props. Be sure to use only those items that are safe, that have no sharp edges and are unbreakable.

• *Kitchen Utensils*—plastic bowl, wooden spoon, wire whisks and cheese grater.

• *Toys*—telephone, vehicle, doll furniture, space weapon, baseball bat, ball, yo-yo, hoola-hoop.

• *Carpenter Tools*—hammer, wrench, screwdriver.

• *Cosmetics and Vanity Items*—powder puff, perfume bottle, shampoo, hairbrush, hand mirror, comb, toothbrush and toothpaste, shaving cream dispenser.

• *Containers*—flower pot, vase, boxes, baskets.

• *Household Items*—dish mop, feather duster, vacuum cleaner hose and nozzle, sponge, clothesline and clothespins, house plants.

• *Novelty Items*—paper or plastic skeletons, pumpkins and other holiday items, oversized pencils, spiders.

• *Stationery Goods*—book, pencil, paintbrush, ruler, rubber band.

• *Pet Supplies*—plastic fishbowl, birdcage, dog bone.

Hammer Prop

Operating the Props.

There are two popular methods for operating props. One technique is to attach them to the end of a coat hanger wire, cardboard towel tube, stick or wood dowel for maneuvering in the playing space onstage. Paint the rod control the same color as the background and it will tend to disappear. Here are some examples of props with rods.

• A *ball* can be thrown back and forth between two characters.

• A *vehicle* can bump along the stage ledge.

• A *sun or moon* can make its appearance in the form of a big arch in the sky to represent the passing of time.

• A *rabbit* can pop out of a magician's hat.

Another method of handling props is to rest an item such as a book or heavy bowl temporarily on the top of the stage's playing board surface if it has one.

Cardboard Car on Stick

Real Ball on Stick

61

Cinderella underwater setting with soap bubbles
(Paper plate puppets on sticks)

THE SHOW'S SURPRISES

The show's surprises—sound effects, music and the illusions—bring magic to a production. A space ship emerges from a whirl of ethereal galaxy dust, a cowboy rides the prairie to the tune of "Home on the Range" and Benjamin Franklin discovers electricity while flying his famous kite in the midst of a terrifying, clapping thunderstorm. There are endless ideas to enhance a show and you will soon find yourself inventing new ones to keep your audience spellbound.

Sound Effects

Whiz, hiss, boom, whistle, toot! A show is also sound. A sound can create images as vividly as a setting. (Much of what we see is frequently associated with what we hear.) Develop a sound track that fits the play and also holds some surprises in store. Commercially recorded sound effects and musical recordings as well as homemade sounds can be used.

If you are a puppet devotee, start a sound department by collecting an array of recordings (cassettes and records), musical instruments and found objects (for homemade sounds) that can enrich your sound ensemble. You may even wish to assign a person to be in charge of sound effects. Store your sound collection in a box or bin labeled "Sound Effects Department."

Mouth Sounds. Sounds you make with your voice produce amazing results. Animal sounds are easy to try. As a starter, think up the different kinds of sounds for a particular animal. For example, a cow could have a variety of *moos*—a long, sad, drawn out moo, a cheerful, happy moo, or a wailing, woeful moo in addition to a barnyard moo! How about trying a dog, cat, duck, mockingbird, and elephant too.

If you are interested in really expanding your vocal sounds, consider investing in *Mouth Sounds* by Frederick R. Newman (order from Puppeteers of America Book Store, P.O. Box 3128, Santa Ana, CA 92703). This super book includes over seventy sounds that can be made vocally, including tugboat blasts, animal calls, trombone glide and cork pop. It even includes a record so you can listen to the sound! With or without the book, do not hesitate to invent sounds of your own.

- *Dentist drill*
- *Train toots*
- *Bubbling soup*
- *Squeaking door*
- *Cuckoo clock*
- *Baby crying*

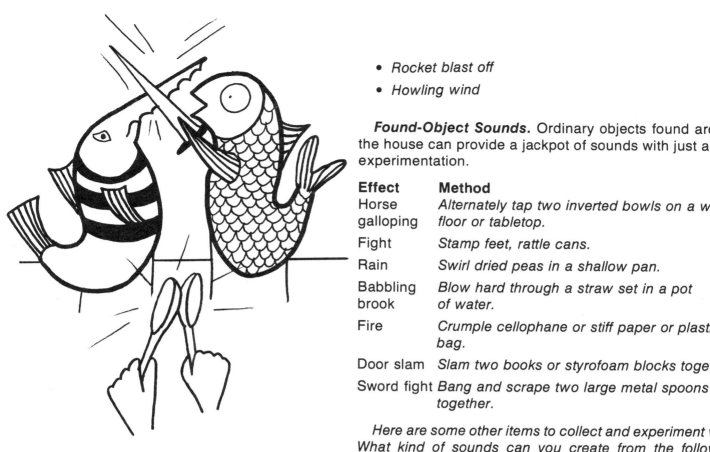

Sword Fight

- *Rocket blast off*
- *Howling wind*

Found-Object Sounds. Ordinary objects found around the house can provide a jackpot of sounds with just a little experimentation.

Effect	Method
Horse galloping	*Alternately tap two inverted bowls on a wood floor or tabletop.*
Fight	*Stamp feet, rattle cans.*
Rain	*Swirl dried peas in a shallow pan.*
Babbling brook	*Blow hard through a straw set in a pot of water.*
Fire	*Crumple cellophane or stiff paper or plastic bag.*
Door slam	*Slam two books or styrofoam blocks together*
Sword fight	*Bang and scrape two large metal spoons together.*

Here are some other items to collect and experiment with. What kind of sounds can you create from the following items? What do the sounds suggest to you?

- *Egg beater*
- *Cheese grater*
- *Wash board*
- *Pliers*
- *Can full of stones*
- *Flour sifter*
- *Wooden spoons*
- *Pot lids*

Recorded Sounds. An excellent addition to your basic collection is the record *101 Sound Effects* by Gateway records (order from Children's Recordings, P.O. Box 11032, Eugene OR 97440). Galloping horses, cheering crowds, vacuum cleaners, grinding crashes and cuckoo clocks are among the many sounds included. Also, ask your local record shop about the sound effect series by Major Records. (If the store does not have these records in stock, they will order one for you from their catalog.) When you are using sound effects records or any records, in fact, you might want to transfer the sounds in order of appearance onto a cassette player for easy handling. Also, consider taping live sounds such as animals. There should be plenty of neighborhood barking dogs to assist you! Sirens, door slams, traffic noise, tractors and construction sounds are also fun to try.

Sea Chanty

Music and Songs

Everyone loves music, whether used for background, song or dance, and its inclusion in a show is a surefire way to win an audience. Music can also help to establish mood during the show.

• *A carnival theme can be marked with calliope or other lively music.*

• *An American Indian tale can have rhythmic drums beating in the background.*

• *A teen club can shake at its foundation with a loud rock number.*

• *An outer space theme can utilize some strange electronic synthesizer tunes.*

• *A royal setting can include heavy, pompous orchestral music.*

• *A seagoing tale would take a lift with some sea ditties.*

You may also wish to call in the resources of a live musician. Almost everyone knows someone who can play an instrument—piano, guitar, flute or other—that would be fun to try.

Musical Instruments. Toy musical instruments or real ones are an asset to your sound collection. Make a search in large discount stores for toy instruments: guitars, whistles, flutes, drums, party noise makers. If you can afford it, invest in rhythm instruments such as cymbals, tambourines, bongo drums, and others.

Songs. Add spark to show with songs. Use a recorded song or create your own songs. If you are not adept at making up tunes, then borrow one. For example, some of those old time favorites can fit many situations by simply changing the wording.

Here are some samples:

• "Here We Go Round the Mulberry Bush"

  "This is the way we pick up pebbles . . ."
  (For "Hansel and Gretel")
  "This is the way I spin some gold . . ."
  (For "Rumpelstiltskin")
  "This is the way we ride to Jupiter . . ."
  (For a science fiction story)

• "Have You Ever Seen a Lassie?"

  "Have you ever seen a goat go trip-trap, go trip-trap . . ."
  (For "The Three Billy Goats Gruff")

Magic Dust

Spouting Whale

- "Jingle Bells"

*"Magic beans, magic beans, magic all the way,
Oh, what fun it is to climb a magic stalk today . . ."*

(For "Jack and the Beanstalk")

Dance. When puppets dance to any tune or song, be sure to give special thought to how the puppet moves to the music. Do not just jiggle it meaninglessly this way and that but choreograph carefully (just like a real Broadway production does!). In fact, watch some live dance groups to get ideas—two steps left, two steps right, then one jump back and one jump forward; twirl around once. There are many interesting patterns which puppets can perform.

Special Effects and Illusions

The audience always remembers the scene in which the soup burned and smoke billowed everywhere, or the one in which the balloon creature blew up so big that it popped! Here is a list of some special effects that heighten the action.

Effect	Method
Smoke, Steam, Fog, Magic dust	*Squeeze sharply a plastic bottle of baby powder.*
Snow	*Throw white confetti*
Spouting Whale	*Water pistol*
Lightning	*Flick lights on and off quickly.*
Circuses, Parties, Other Festivities	*Throw colored confetti and streamers.*
Scarey Eyes	*Brightly colored eye shapes can appear to dance in the dark if attached to sticks painted black which are moved about in front of a black background.*
Launching Rocket Ship	*Design a rocketship in two sections and attach each section to a separate stick. Bring the two sections together for the rocket's launching, then split them apart as it orbits in space.*

Other Surprises to Pull from Your Sleeve

The puppet theater is illusionary and can create a world of fantasy and magic. Your imagination has no limit when trying out illusions which can be one of the most enjoyable aspects of the show. Plan to include as many of these surprises as possible. Here are some more tricks to create.

Effect	Method
Expanding Bread	*A loaf of bread baked by the witch in "Hansel and Gretel" could appear to go wayward. Cut out an extra long, billowy shape of cardboard or foam. Color it to look like dough. Poke the tip out a swinging oven door and gradually extend it to its full length.*
Growing Plant	*A vegetable or flower can slowly extend up from the ground to its full height by means of a stick attached to the prop.*

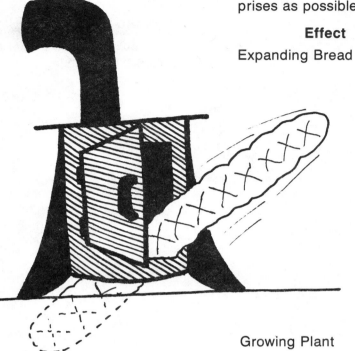

Party Blower

Tape a horn or party blower to a length of narrow plastic tubing (obtained at hardware store) and insert the tube through a hole in the puppet's mouth. The tube can be hidden inside the puppet and blown from backstage.)

Turn-Around Character

A turn-around-puppet that has a different face painted on each side of it can be intriguing. For example, a happy and sad one, or a "Dr. Jekyll and Mr. Hyde" character.

Exploding Balloon Puppet

Draw features onto a balloon with felt-tip marker pens; stretch the neck of the balloon over a length of narrow plastic tubing and tape it in place. Blow up balloon through tube until puppet explodes (or pop balloon with a pin).

Split Apart Characters

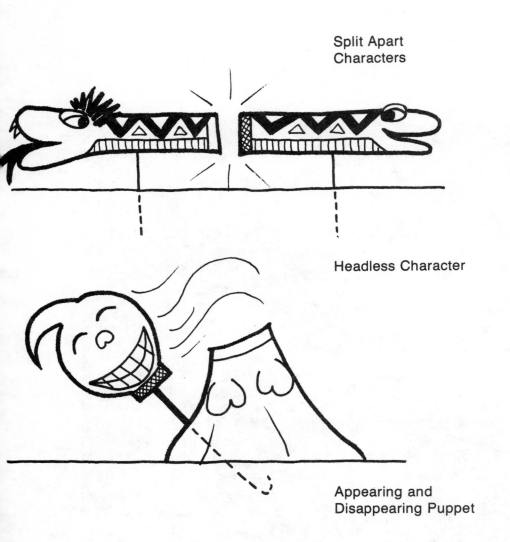

A snake or worm can split apart (perhaps the front and back end have had a disagreement) and come back together again (after making up) if the puppet is made in two sections which are attached with Velcro® .

Headless Character

The head of a ghost or monster character can actually come off the character's body section for a chilling effect in the same manner as above.

Appearing and Disappearing Puppet

An awesome genie or extra terrestrial creature can appear out of a magic urn or other vessel when rubbed. The character can be attached to a stick and hidden behind the urn, then popped up on cue, then down.

If you think you are running out of ideas, then just take a reach up one of your sleeves and see what else you find. As a devoted puppeteer, you are undoubtedly a great illusionist as well; just the thing needed to keep your audience in wonder.

The cast takes that final step into the world of theater

(Nancy Renfro and friends)

★★★★★★★★★★★★★★★★★★★★★★★★★★★★★★★★★★★★

Staging The Show

At last you have all the show's components together: the script, puppets, scenery, props, surprises, the entire ensemble. The real fun is just ahead as you take that final step into the world of theater and meet your audience.

TAPED OR LIVE SHOWS

One of the first things you must decide is whether you will want to tape the show or perform it live. Both methods have their advantages and disadvantages so it will be a personal choice.

A Taped Show can have interesting prerecorded music and sound effects all set to go. However, with a taped show you will have to practice *very* diligently so that the puppets' actions are in perfect timing with the dialogue, so as not to break the illusion or to make the puppets appear silly.

Be sure in taping shows you have the best quality tape recorder that can be obtained. Possibly consider renting one from a local audio equipment supplier. Also, tape voices in a room relatively free from outside noises. A carpeted room will have better acoustics than one without a carpet. Experiment and make some tests by speaking into the microphone to see how close or far voices should be to the microphone.

A live show is more spontaneous and you will have complete control over the timing of the puppets' actions with the voice. Also with a live show you can change the show as you go along. Audience participation can be used freely since you will not need to worry about following a tape.

In either case, whether taped or live, the most crucial thing is that the dialogue and other sounds be distinct enough to be heard in the back of the room as well as the front. In live performances, be sure that your enunciation is clear and your voice is loud since sound can be easily muffled behind the stage's curtain. Place the tape recorder speakers in front of the stage, in a central location, facing the audience. Always test out the tapes and live voices beforehand and have someone listen from various areas of the room.

THE STAGE

In every aspect the stage should be an asset to the puppeteer, not a hindrance. If you plan to travel about with your show, you will want a lightweight and portable stage

for ease in transporting; also it may need to collapse to fit in a vehicle. On the other hand, if the stage is to be part of a permanent fixture in a room mobility is not necessary.

Simple Stages

If your goals are to put on a simple and informal puppet show, an instant stage is perfectly acceptable.

• *A turned over table.* Turn a table over with the surface facing the audience. If desired cover the table's surface with fabric. Scenery can also be taped onto the surface, if desired.

• *Cutting Board Stage.* Purchased at a fabric shop, a cutting board makes an ideal portable stage. Open it out and stand it on a table top or floor.

• *A Board Stage.* A four to six feet long board can provide a simple stage with great portability and the added benefit of a playing board on which to rest props. Staple a piece of fabric along the front edge. Lay the boards between two chairs or tables for support.

• *Appliance boxes.* This versatile stage can be fashioned from refrigerator or other large appliance carton. Window holes of any shape can be cut into the carton for a performing area. The back wall should be partially cut out to allow the puppeteer to enter inside. Paint or decorate the carton to suit the show's theme: circus tent, Arctic landscape, solar system, forest or other.

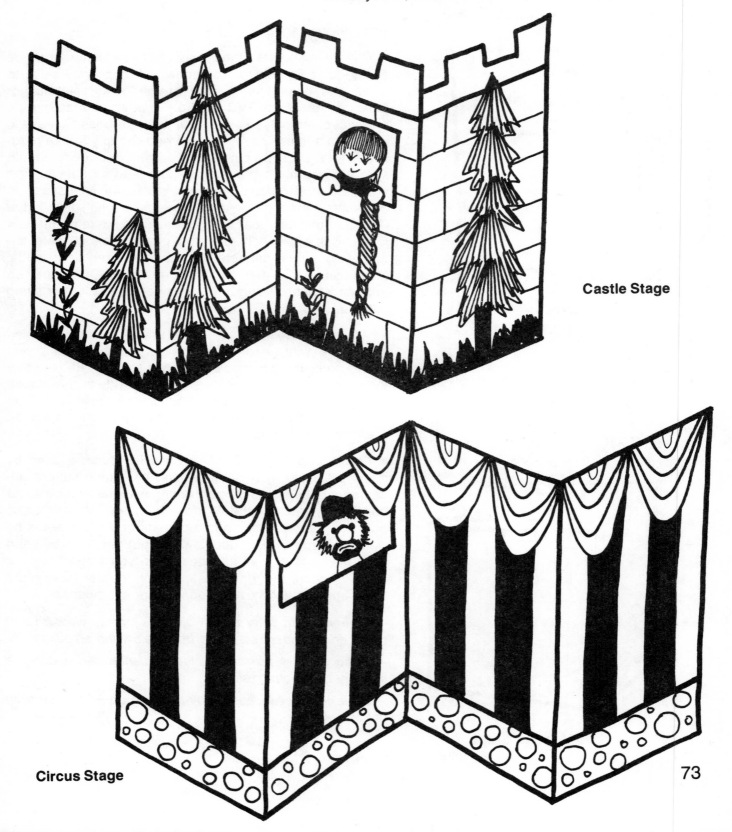

Castle Stage

Circus Stage

73

A clothespin scenery holder as described in the section on scenery can be attached to any of the above stages to hold moveable scenic pieces.

If you need a background for any of the above stages, use a wall or set up a panel or collapsible movie screen behind the stage. Background scenery can then be hung on these panels.

Advanced Stages

A more elaborate stage for formal productions can be easily built. Search for someone with carpentry skills to assist the construction. One of the best materials for building stages is PVC piping. This white plastic pipe material commonly used for plumbing purposes is easy to work with and can easily be obtained cheaply from a hardware store. It can be cut with a hacksaw or other fine tooth saw. An assortment of matching elbows to connect the vertical and horizontal tube members make it possible to assemble almost any kind of stage. A special solvent glue (for adult use only) can be purchased to make permanent joints. Use a ½ inch diameter pipe for small table top stages, a 1 inch diameter for medium sized floor model stages and 2 inch diameter for large stages. There are two popular styles of stages to consider before undertaking construction.

Window Opening Stage

• *Window Opening Stage.* In this most commonly used stage, the window often has a curtain that opens and closes so scenery can be changed in secrecy. Be sure that the window opening is at least four feet wide to give ample room for puppets to move about freely. (Beware, for so often the window opening in this type stage is too small an area for action to occur.)

• *Open Style Stage.* This less familiar style is used by many professional puppeteers and has some superb advantages. The space for performing is usually much wider (four to six feet) than the Window Opening Stage and gives puppets greater freedom to move about. Also, there is no window frame to obstruct views so puppets can be seen from the front as well as sides. This type stage does not usually feature a curtain. Also, certain theater tricks need to be applied when using puppets; for example:

—*A puppet can enter or exit by appearing to walk up and down an imaginary staircase from below the stage.*

—*Since there is no curtain, the audience can watch the scenery being changed.*

—*Or, a puppet can appear by popping up and down from below stage.*

Open Style Stage

Playing Board

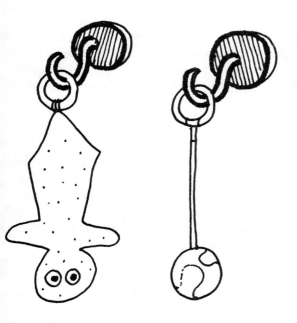

Puppet and Prop Holders

A top quality Open Style stage can be purchased from Nancy Renfro Studios. It is a puppeteer's dream in that it collapses down to a compact 36 x 10 x 10" size for easy storage and carrying. It also features handy magnet scenery holders and attachable lights. For free information, write Nancy Renfro Studios, 1117 W. 9th Street, Austin, TX 78703.

With either type stage, the Window or Open Style Stage, it is recommended that the stage is high enough so that the performers can *stand* while operating the puppets. This places the puppets high, allowing the audience a better view in a large room. This position also gives puppeteers maximum freedom and energy to move about. Sitting in a chair certainly is more comfortable, but very restricting. However, when giving shows in a small room, such as a classroom, a stage at seating or kneeling height may be preferred so the audience will not crane necks to look up at puppets.

Special Stage Features

Some special features follow that will make your stage more serviceable.

• *A Playing Board.* This horizontal 3-5 inch wide board lies flat on the front edge of the stage area and serves as the puppets' "floor." It is handy to place props and scenery, such as a book or toy telephone, on this surface.

• *Scenery Holder.* This can be attached to the inside edge of the playing board or stage itself for holding cardboard movable scenic pieces such as a tree, house, or volcano. Several types of scenery holders are described in the section on scenery construction.

• *Puppet and Prop Holders.* Cup hooks can be attached to the inside of the stage for hanging puppets and props. Sew or tape large curtain rings onto the hems of puppets or props to hang onto the hooks. A narrow shelf midway down the stage, inside, is useful for holding other loose items.

• *Fabric Covering.* Fabric used to cover the front of the stage should be durable and heavy enough so light does not show through. Black, gray, dark blue or deep purple are common colors that do not to distract from the puppets. Robe fleece, velour, velvet, textured polyester knit, or other nonwrinkle matte finish fabrics are recommended. (Fabrics with a sheen will reflect light.) A string of simple drapery pom-pom trim or fringe across the bottom or middle of the fabric will give it a festive touch.

• *Window Curtain.* Any festive fabric would highlight a Window Opening Stage and add a gay touch to the production. A curtain can open and close if attached to a draw-drapery rod.

• *Background Cover.* A solid piece of fabric hung on the background of the stage can be a permanent part of the stage setup. Choose a basic color that will complement the show. Black is often used but tends to produce a heavy and sometimes brooding effect which sometimes may be desired. A sky blue, however, is a very appealing all purpose color, especially for everyday scenes and is a flattering color for most skin tones. Polyester felts, double-knits or velours (which do not wrinkle) make good background fabrics.

• *Lighting.* Soft light may be needed backstage so that the puppeteers can see, and a single low watt lamp should be sufficient. For spotlights, almost any lamp can be used: theatrical spots, floodlights, large flashlights, desk lamps, overhead shadow projector light, or consider a simple clip-on shade purchased at a hardware store. Spotlights facing stage openings can be placed on a table, hung on walls, or attached to a chair or stand. Be sure to test out bulbs beforehand so that they are not too hot for the lamp type. Experiment and relocate lights to see what works best for your set up and view puppets with lights critically from various locations in the audience. A self contained dimmer switch unit (hardware store) is a bonus to have backstage to control lights.

REHEARSING THE SHOW

The roar of the crowd and smell of greasepaint is just a short distance away. Now it's time to buckle down into the most challenging part of show business. Be sure you have allowed plenty of time for this part of the production.

Here are some ideas for organizing rehearsals:

• *A director would be helpful for leading the show to a successful premiere.* This person could be an extra member of the troupe, or if the show is done in a class or other group, then the instructor. The director can keep a sharp watch from out front, while the cast rehearses, guiding the puppets' actions and watching for stage blunders, such as puppets that sink too low or voices that are not loud enough. Also, the director can help cue puppeteers backstage during the performance for forgotten lines or props.

• *If members in the group do not already have parts, why not have tryouts!* The best actors should be the leads, and everyone should agree on this for the success of the show. A confident loud voice is essential.

- *Before rehearsing, have a script reading jam session without puppets.* It is important that everyone becomes familiar with the play. One of the biggest problems in script reading during the play is that the puppeteer can get bogged down reading the words and lines and forget to move the puppets. So the more familiar everyone is with the script, the better.
- *Scripts can be hung backstage for puppeteers to refer to.* If the script is attached to a clip board with the bottoms of pages stapled together, each page can be flipped downward as needed.
- *Next, organize all the props, puppets, and puppeteers backstage in order of appearance.* Also think about how characters will enter and exit. Block out these actions with the group beforehand so everyone has a basic idea of what to do.
- *Keep some emergency items handy*—stapler, pins, or tape—backstage for meeting any unexpected crisis, such as a feature that falls off a puppet.
- *Consider all aspects of the play when rehearsing.* Not only must the group rehearse the puppets' parts but they must rehearse putting props and scenery on and off stage as well as synchronizing sound and special effects. Plan which members of the group will take care of these items.

The actual number of planned rehearsals will depend mainly on how much you wish to perfect the show. Three rehearsals would be a minimum number, but more would be required if a top notch play is the goal.

First Rehearsal is the warm-up to get everyone familiar with the play. Divide the play into sections and practice each section separately. Feel relaxed acting with the puppets. If it is an improvised story, then make up the parts as you go along. Keep the dialogue free and talk up a storm! (You can always cut later.) The first rehearsal is often twice as long as the last.

Middle Rehearsals allow you to gradually improve the play. After a brainstorming session with the group, you may want to make some changes to firm up the script—shorten dialogue, add a new punch line for one that didn't come off as expected, etc. Remain flexible right up to the final performance. Continue to rehearse the play in segments until each segment has all the kinks worked out of it. Concentrate on lively speech and making sure the puppets are showing off their true personalities.

Dress Rehearsal should be a run-through of the entire play, linking all the segments together. Most important, be sure voices are loud enough to be heard and puppets are not sinking low and are moving when they should be (and *not* moving when they shouldn't). All props and special effects are included at this session. Pretend that this is the real thing.

★★★★★★★★★★★★★★★★★★★★★★★★★★★★★★★★★

Show Time!

Lights, curtain . . . action! Your world premiere should be an event to remember. Excite people beforehand about the show. You might even give your troupe a special name to distinguish it—Popcorn Puppet Theater, The Wacky Wonder World Puppets, the Inner-Galactic Space Puppet Theater or other.

PASS THE WORD

Think of some unique ways to let people know about the coming performance:

- *Tack up colorful posters in the area.*
- *Pass out bookmarks with the show dates.*
- *Distribute balloons in the neighborhood with a tag telling about your show attached to the string.*
- *Have someone walk up and down a busy pedestrian area wearing a placard advertising the show.*
- *Send an article about the show to the local newspaper or radio station.*
- *Approach your local cable television station to feature parts of your show to spark interest.*
- *Give out freebies advertising the show, such as a silver star for an outer space show, paper skull for a Halloween horror tale, or peppermint candy from the Witch's house for "Hansel and Gretel."*

PLANNING THE PERFORMANCE

There are a number of ways to increase the popularity of your performance. You might wish to include one of the following ideas.

- *Related Activity at the Show.*   Since a play may last only fifteen minutes to a half hour, an additional activity might be scheduled. Some possibilities are: a refreshment break, games, sing along with a puppet, a performance by a musical, mime or dance group, a story-telling session, a magic trick, or a puppet-making demonstration.

- *Star Appearances.*   One way of unifying a play is to introduce a leading puppet character—such as an announcer, joker, riddle man, or magician.

- *Audience Participation.*   An audience enjoys communicating with a puppet and becoming part of the show. It can be great fun for everyone. Here are three variations on this idea:

—*The puppet can ask the audience questions during a question period or when he wants the audience to help him solve a problem. For example, when Red Riding Hood says, "What big teeth you have, Grandma!" The Wolf could turn to the audience and ask them what to say. Unfamiliar situations can also be handled this way.*

—*The audience can ask the puppet questions. Many TV personalities today have informal question periods, and a puppet could, too.*

—*Puppet and audience may participate together. For example, the audience can help a puppet count down for a rocket launch, repeat magic words, cheers, etc.*

CURTAIN TIME!

The first impression for the audience entering the theater should be exciting: dimmed lights, waiting stage, music. Try to start on time. As soon as the audience is settled, switch off the lights. Curtain up and begin!

Roll right through your first show with complete confidence. There are mistakes in all shows, and most of the time the audience won't even notice. Some mistakes turn out to be quite funny (a puppet's head falling off or a prop tumbling into the audience), so make a comment and capitalize on the situation! (A puppet can easily pretend that the blunder was part of the act and ask someone in the audience to help out.)

The big reward comes with the final applause and the feeling that the audience has had a great time. Come on out and take a big bow.

Congratulations, you've broken a leg!